T0368387

Handbook for Righteous Living

William E. Summers III

WESTBOW
P R E S S®
A DIVISION OF THOMAS NELSON
& ZONDERVAN

WestBow Press books may be ordered through booksellers or by contacting:

WestBow Press
A Division of Thomas Nelson & Zondervan
1663 Liberty Drive
Bloomington, IN 47403
www.westbowpress.com
844-714-3454

ISBN: 979-8-3850-3466-6 (sc)
ISBN: 979-8-3850-3465-9 (e)

Library of Congress Control Number: 2024920421

Print information available on the last page.

WestBow Press rev. date: 10/01/2024

This book is dedicated to the late
Dr. Charles F. Stanley
of
In Touch Ministries
Whose words of wisdom
Through God's Holy Spirit
Inspired me to write:
Handbook for Righteous Living

CONTENTS

CONTENTS

PREFACE

Has humanity lost its way? Are we confused about who we are and why we are here? The one characteristic that makes us dominant over the rest of creation is that God gave man the capacity to think and to reason. And yet we as a people have all these thoughts that we are somehow different from God's original creation. Have we lost our moral compass? Those "things" that were once considered bad or taboo are now acceptable; that which was once considered wrong is now all right. Do you really need examples? Just look around you! What happened? I believe that if you are fed something long enough, you tend to go along with it or "Buy into it!" You become desensitized to it. That does not make it right, just "acceptable." I could get into laws and regulations that have brought about changes in our society over the past 40 years, but that is not the purpose or intent of this book. All that I am asking is that you, the reader, do a little soul-searching.

How do you measure up morally today? Do you join

the crowd, anything goes, who cares as long as no one gets hurt, "Just Do It?" Do you weigh both sides of the issue at hand and make your decision based on the evidence? Are you so stuck in your ways such that right is right and wrong is wrong, and there is no other option? Or do you bend or sway to follow the crowd? It depends on your moral values. If your morals are strong, rooted in God and country, you will make decisions that are based on knowledge and an understanding of your surroundings. If you can be swayed and would prefer to be a little stronger in your faith and commitments, then perhaps this book is for you. There is an old saying which goes, "You can lead a horse to water, but you can't make him drink." In other words, all the preaching in the world will not save the soul that does not want to seek change and lead a better life.

None of us like to change, but sometimes we look inwardly and tell ourselves that something just is not right. I am not happy with myself. I do not like the me I see. I wish I were more like so-and-so: richer, smarter, more successful, more beautiful or handsome. Believe me, I understand! I have asked myself these very same questions over the years and ended up with the same answer…would such a change have made a difference?

The very same words that I am about to share with you in the following chapters are the words that contributed to the adjustments which I made that changed my course in life. Never for a moment believe that I am "Holier than thou!" Be not deceived! Know that we all have habits! We are creatures of habit; but we need to make sure we develop "good habits" and positive attributes that complement our Father in Heaven.

INTRODUCTION

The greatest aspect of our human nature is to know God and our Lord and Savior, Jesus Christ, on a personal level. Our spiritual growth in that knowledge defines who we are...our character. Love for others and love of self grows out of this desire to know God. When we begin to understand this reality, we may begin to understand who we are, why we are here, and what our purpose is in life. Herein is the reason I wrote <u>Handbook for Righteous Living</u>, that we all may draw nearer to God, The Father, and truly understand His principles, and how these principles relate to our life.

Our Heavenly Father has assured us of eternal life through His son, Jesus Christ. Jesus bore our sins and the sins of the world on the cross so that we might have everlasting life. This life after death is given to each of us through God's salvation. When we humble ourselves before Jesus and ask that our sins be forgiven, The Father hears our plea; and because of His love and mercy, He forgives us of our transgressions, cleanses us of our sins, and sets us on a path to a new life. The key is that we believe that a change is taking place…that we have faith in Jesus; and that God will do what He has promised us.

Once you begin to live by what is called the fruit of the Spirit, you will begin to enjoy life in a unique way. The Bible tells us that the old is passed away, and our life becomes new. The burden of sin that has plagued our life for years should begin to fade away. It will not be easy, but those who commit themselves to living this new life will begin to experience a change in attitude and behavior. Situations will become easier to control, your burden will become lighter, and the petty things that used to annoy and frustrate you will begin to pass. Let me share a little story with you.

My journey is not so much different than most Christians. I grew up in a small Methodist Church, believed in God and Jesus Christ, and often felt close to God in my adolescent years. But life has a way of pulling us away. I have had doubts myself about the existence of God; but when I have seen His power and authority working miracles in my life that I cannot explain, I have no doubt in a higher power beyond the scope of all that we are able to comprehend. We have all struggled with our sinful nature; but if we cannot control our desire to sin, it can grow into a habit that is extremely hard to break. Unfortunately, we have done what *we* want for so long, that the road to recovery is more bewildering when we attempt to find our way back home.

I was fortunate enough at the age of sixty-five to finally find that path to righteous living. As I sat in a local church on Palm Sunday in 2012, the ending of <u>The Passion of the Christ</u> was shown on the big screen just prior to the service.

I had never seen the movie. But as I watched, I was moved with compassion when I saw how Jesus Christ was treated by the crowd as He made His way to Calvery. I wept! I choked back the tears; but I was moved emotionally to think that Jesus gave His life on the cross so that I might have eternal life. If He would lay down His life for me, a sinner, then why am I not living my life for Him?

You see! It is never too late in life to ask forgiveness for our sins. God, out of His patience, love, and mercy for us, is always ready to forgive us so that we might be redeemed. Even after we are truly saved, we may still have the desire to sin. It is not easy to change directions overnight after years of sinful behavior. However, for those who are serious and are dedicated to a new life, it is essential that we turn to God and ask Him to come into our life; seek His word through the Bible; study a daily devotional; attend a church that preaches the true word of God by following scripture; and pray without ceasing. Be determined to fight the devil, because he feels that your salvation is a welcome invitation to disrupt your life in every way possible.

As a result of following the above steps myself, I began to watch Dr. Charles Stanley on TV, and I began to pursue a different path. In December of 2012, I ordered my first devotional from his ministry which I still faithfully receive and study daily. Consequently, in January 2021, I received a calendar. Each month provided an inspirational message from Dr. Stanley and a Bible verse on the back side of the calendar. Opposite the page was a section to list "Prayers, Goals, and Notes." I used that page instead to write down Bible verses, particularly Bible verses that listed "ways" that I could begin to change my life through meditating on and memorizing scripture. I began to grow spiritually, and my mind and my thoughts began to change. I developed a whole new attitude toward life in general. God has planted a seed in my heart; and now I want to share it with you so that you might grow in your relationship with God, the Father, and Jesus Christ, our Lord. I want to share the joy that I experience every day and the newness of life that God has offered me.

I would like to believe in my heart that this handbook is for everyone: for those who are lost and might, otherwise, never know God's grace; for those who had a relationship with God but have fallen away; for those who you feel that something is not quite right in your life, and you are searching for an answer; and even for those of you who are already saved, I pray that you may be strengthened through this study of God's word. Whatever the reason, may you come to Jesus Christ and seek His loving mercy and grace.

May your journey begin here and now!

It is no secret what God can do.
What He's done for others
He'll do for you.
With arms wide open
He'll pardon you.
It is no secret
What God can do.

(STUART HAMBLEN: SEE APPENDIX D)

CHAPTER 1

DO YOU HAVE THE FRUIT OF THE SPIRIT?

"Live a life worthy of the Lord and please Him in every way, bearing fruit in every good work, growing in the knowledge of God, being strengthened with all power according to His glorious might so that you may have great endurance and patience, and giving joyful thanks to the Father, who has qualified you to share in the inheritance of His holy people in the Kingdom of light."

COLOSSIANS 1:10-12

What does the Bible mean when it says, "We should bear fruit in every good work." We might use the comparison of any plant that bears fruit, an apple tree for example. If that plant receives adequate rainfall, sunlight, the proper nutrients, and insecticide, then that plant will be healthy and will grow strong. And the fruit that is produced will be of average size or better, succulent, and free of defect such as bugs or disease. However, if that same apple tree does not receive the proper nurturing, the tree may become weak, the yield or production might be poor, and the apples could be infested with insects, disease, and the like.

The same can be said about each of us. If we are strengthened through God's power, we can develop a patience and endurance that carries us through the tough times in life. On the other hand, if we don't receive spiritual nourishment through God's Holy Word (The Bible), surround ourselves with like-minded individuals who have a strong values system, and grow spiritually through prayer (seeking a personal relationship with the Father), we too can become weak in spirit and backslide without any knowledge of what is really happening in our life. So, the fruit of the Spirit helps us to grow in our spiritual life.

Do you have the fruit of the Spirit? I have listed each of the characteristics which constitute the fruit of the Spirit below with a synopsis from my most recent In Touch devotional. Check yourself out!

1. **Love** is the foundation for all other virtues. We cultivate it by embracing God's unconditional love for us.
2. **Joy** is contentment regardless of our circumstances.
3. **Peace** comes from trusting God and surrendering to Him.
4. **Patience** (Long Suffering, Endurance) is developed by trusting His perfect timing.

5. **Kindness** (Forgiveness) is God's compassion reflected to others.

6. **Goodness** (To do what is right) occurs as we mirror His righteousness and justice.

7. **Faithfulness** means we are steadfast and trustworthy.

8. **Gentleness** (Meekness, Lack of Anger) comes when we approach others with humility.

9. **Self-Control** (Temperance) requires us to exercise restraint and rely on the Holy Spirit's strength.

Now you might ask, why use the singular word "fruit?" "Fruit" suggests that we consider all nine qualities as belonging together. We cannot choose the ones we want and discard the rest. All nine qualities are a part of the one fruit…a part of the whole! For example, if we are found to be weak in any of the above characteristics, then we need to develop that area of our character. We need to practice being loving, joyful, and kind toward others if we find it difficult to love others. Likewise, we cannot enjoy peace, love, and joy if we are lacking in our patience with others. Or we may find it difficult to be faithful to others if we lack self-control. We recognize the righteous by their fruit. The Bible tells us that Jesus is the vine, and we are the branches. Thus, any branch that does not bear fruit will be pruned or cut off from salvation. Only in God and through God is there real meaning to our life and a reason to live.

I am sure that you have heard the old cliché, "You can count the number of seeds in an apple, but only God can count the number of apples in a seed." Likewise, He has planted His seed of knowledge in each of us. Each seed is designed to grow within us to fulfill God's plan for our life. We can either grow and develop as we seek His word and live according to His will; or we can wither and die spiritually from the lack of nurturing that He offers to every one of us.

> In John 13:34-35, Jesus said, "A new command I give you: Love one another. As I have loved you, so you must love one another. By this everyone will know that you are my disciples if you love one another."

> Again, Jesus said, "By their fruit you will recognize them. Do people pick grapes from thornbushes, or figs from thistles? Likewise, every good tree bears good fruit, but a bad tree bears bad fruit. A good tree cannot bear bad fruit, and a bad tree cannot bear good fruit. Every tree that does not bear good fruit is cut down and thrown into the fire. Thus, by their fruit you will recognize them" (Matt.7:16-20). Thus, we are to strive daily in our walk with God to be filled with the fruit of the Spirit.

SOMETHING TO CONSIDER:

All pleasure, work, achievements, wealth, relationships are meaningless without the presence of God to fill us with Fruit of the Spirit and to give us eternal life. Only in God and through God is there meaning to life... a true meaning to live!

CHAPTER 2

WALKING DAILY WITH THE HELP OF GOD

"No temptation has overtaken you except what is common to mankind. And God is faithful; He will not let you be tempted beyond what you can bear. But when you are tempted, He will also provide a way out so that you can endure it."

1 CORINTHIANS 10:13

Are you "Walking with God," interacting with God throughout the course of a day, feeling His presence and power, and receiving His strength and guidance? What is your relationship with Jesus like? Do you love Him; call on Him in time of need; speak to Him daily; thank Him for taking your place on the cross? Or do you ignore Him, give no thought to Jesus throughout the day; fail to serve Him in your love for others; curse His name and fail to recognize Him as the Son of God? How we treat Him today is how He will remember us tomorrow.

Jesus said, "Ask and it will be given you; seek and you will find; knock and the door will be opened to you. For everyone who asks receives; the one who seeks finds; and to the one who knocks, the door will be opened" (Matt 7:7-8). Oftentimes in life, we do not receive God's promises because we do not ask. But simply asking is not enough. We must believe that our prayers will be answered. It is essential that we seek Him so that we might find the answer to our desires. Figuratively speaking, we knock at the door, and in His immense wisdom and power, He hears our prayer and opens the door. Lastly, wait! Be patient such that your request might be granted. God may not answer right away, but He knows our needs and will always provide an outcome that is best for each of His children.

Rest assured, if there any evil thought or desire toward others, or if we should ask in a selfish manner, seeking self-reward, or if we are not truthful and righteous in our request, God will shut the door! Our thoughts and desires must be pure and with good intent.

Regardless of how you answered the above questions, there are ten thoughts we should consider in our daily walk with God. "Whoever does these things will never be shaken." (Ps. 15:2-5). And while we are at it, let us dive a little deeper into each characteristic listed to gain a better perspective on its meaning:

1. To walk without <u>blame:</u> Sinless, without any wrongdoing, innocent of any wrong.
2. To do what is <u>righteous</u> in God's eyes: Morally right or justifiable, virtuous.
3. To speak the <u>truth</u> from the heart: Honesty, reliability, credibility.
4. To avoid <u>slander</u> of others: False or defamatory oral statement about a person.
5. To do no <u>wrong</u> to my neighbor: Hurtful, slander, gossip.
6. To cast no <u>slurs</u> on others: An insinuation or allegation about someone that is likely to insult them or damage their reputation.
7. To despise the <u>vile</u> and the <u>wicked</u>, but honor those who fear the Lord: Vile-extremely unpleasant; wicked-evil, morally wrong.
8. To keep my <u>oaths</u>, even when it hurts, and not change my mind: Unwavering, marked by firm determination or resolution.
9. To <u>lend money</u> to the poor without interest: Generosity, genuine, an unselfish act.
10. To refuse any <u>bribe</u> against the innocent: Trading fame or fortune for a lie.

Living righteously will depend on how closely we adhere to these principles in our life. Understand, no matter how hard we try, there is no one who will ever be able to follow each step daily. Jesus was the only human being to ever walk this earth in complete obedience to the Father. But the more that we work to improve each step, the closer we will come to improving our walk with

God; and the easier it will become to talk with God as you continue to grow spiritually.

Remember, God is always ready and able to help us if we are willing to come to Him in prayer and listen for His answer. Listening is essential to walking with God.

> "But be very careful to keep the commandment and the law that Moses the servant of the Lord gave you: to love the Lord your God, to walk in obedience to Him, to keep His commands, to hold fast to Him and to serve Him with all your heart and with all your soul" (Jos. 22:5).

SOMETHING TO CONSIDER:

The Lord commissions Christians to carry the Word to those who are hurting, to those who need encouragement, to those who do not understand, or to those who may be lost. We do not have to be a Bible scholar to deliver God's word and teach others. Who can you reach out to today to offer a word of encouragement, comfort, or healing?

CHAPTER 3

WALKING AS CHILDREN OF LIGHT

**"Follow God's example, therefore, as dearly
loved children and walk in the way of love, just
as Christ loved us and gave Himself up for us as
a fragrant offering and sacrifice to God."**

EPHESIANS 5:1-2

The question is, how shall we walk to become "Children of Light?"

1. "Live as children of light (for the fruit of the light consists in all goodness, righteousness, and truth) and find out what pleases the Lord. Have nothing to do with the fruitless deeds of darkness, but rather expose them. It is shameful even to mention what the disobedient do in secret. But everything exposed

by the light becomes visible and everything that is illuminated becomes a light." (Eph. 5:9-13)

2. "Among you there must not be even a hint of sexual immorality, or of any kind of impurity, or of greed, because these are improper for God's holy people. Nor should there be obscenity, foolish talk, or coarse joking, which are out of place, but rather thanksgiving. For you can be sure: No immoral, impure, or greedy person, such a person is an idolater, has any inheritance in the kingdom of Christ and of God. Let no one deceive you with empty words, for because of such things God's wrath comes on those who are disobedient." (Eph. 5:3-6)

3. "Be very careful, then, how you live, not as unwise but as wise, making the most of every opportunity, because the days are evil. Therefore, do not be foolish, but understand what the Lord's will is." (Eph. 5:15-17)

4. "Be filled with the Spirit, speaking to one another with psalms, hymns, and songs from the Spirit. Sing and make music from the heart to the Lord, always giving thanks to God the Father for everything in the name of our Lord Jesus Christ." (Eph. 5:19-20)

If we are to be children of light, bearing the fruit of the Spirit, and walking in the light of the Holy Spirit, we will not be bound by the trappings of those who are of a sinful nature. Sexual immorality, other impurities, and greed become the mark of the sinner. Using coarse language and foolish talk, even crass jokes are unbecoming of those who would call themselves followers of Jesus Christ. The

Lord despises obscene gestures and all kinds of foolishness and disobedience.

Therefore, walk as children of the light, filled with the Holy Spirit. When we fall into temptation, and we all do (because we are only human), we must turn to God in prayer, and/or recite those verses of scripture that are close to our heart. By doing so, we can ward off evil and draw closer to God. When we become weak in the Spirit, Satan wants nothing more than to enter the door to our heart. However, pure light casts out sin!

As loving and compassionate as our God is, He is intolerant of those who do evil. He is no respecter of persons. He has no mercy for the sinner. We are all born into the world as sinners. And sin in our life becomes habit if we allow that sin to grow and fester. Sin is damning! Sin condemns us and damages our life. Sin distances us from God and from Jesus Christ. The only escape is to seek salvation through Jesus Christ. (I will share how you can become saved in Chapter 14: Pray for Continued Salvation).

> "This is the message we have heard from Him and declare to you: God is light; in Him there is no darkness at all. If we claim to have fellowship with Him and yet walk in the darkness, we lie and do not live out the truth. But if we walk in the light, as he is in the light, we have fellowship with one another, and the blood of Jesus, His Son, purifies us from all sin." (1 John 1:5-7)

SOMETHING TO CONSIDER:

Overcoming our human frailties: Where there is light, there can be no darkness. Where God reigns, Satan cannot gain a foothold. Jesus is the light of the world, and we are children of that light. Therefore, allow no darkness to enter and possess the corners of your mind.

CHAPTER 4

ADMONITIONS FOR HOLY LIVING

"Make every effort to add to your faith goodness; and to goodness, knowledge; and to knowledge, self-control; and to self-control, perseverance; and to perseverance, godliness; and to godliness, mutual affection; and to mutual affection, love. For if you possess these qualities in increasing measure, they will keep you from being ineffective and unproductive in your knowledge of our Lord Jesus Christ."

2 PETER 3:5-8

The term admonition can mean many things. Admonitions here means instruction, recommendation, guidance, and direction. Hence, listed here are the Admonitions for Holy Living as presented in (1 Thes. 5:12-22):

LIVING IN PEACE WITH EACH OTHER:

When we speak of living in peace with each other, living in peace with every human being comes to mind. Race, color, or religious preference should not hold us back from loving others and being at peace with them. Every human being lives and breathes the same as you and I do. We all have feelings; we all have our strengths and weaknesses. And yet God has created every one of us in His own image but different in character. We should be able to accept one another, as we are, for who we are, and without prejudice.

"Turn from evil and do good, seek peace and pursue it." (Ps. 34:14)

WARN THOSE WHO ARE IDLE AND DISRUPTIVE:

You may have heard the phrase, "Idle hands are the Devil's workshop." Quite often, those who are idle seem to have time to think about and create mischief. Those idle thoughts can range from pulling a harmless prank on others to something of a more serious nature. I am reminded of a teacher in the classroom reprimanding a student for disruptive behavior. That behavior is intolerable if the teacher is to have order, control the classroom, and gain the attention of their fellow students. Warning those who are disorderly helps to achieve a calmer, more manageable atmosphere. Protests and demonstrations can easily get out of control and incite others to become agitated. Eventually, situations can progress to the point of total chaos, whereas calmer minds may have prevailed and prevented an awkward situation.

"In the name of the Lord Jesus Christ, we command you, brothers and sisters, to keep away from every believer who is idle and disruptive and does not live according to the teaching you received from us." (2 Thes. 3:6)

ENCOURAGE THE DISHEARTENED:

All of us at one time or another can feel down and depressed, stressed from life's troubles, weakened by situations that are out of our control, and lacking in faith because we fail to see a way out. Isn't it comforting when someone unexpectedly consoles us and reminds us that things will be all right? We can each lift others up by a positive word and a caring attitude. As Robert Schuller, pastor of Garden Grove Church in California used to say, "Tough times never last, but tough people do." He authored a book entitled the <u>Peak to Peek Principle</u> which discussed the peaks and valleys that we face in life. When we are on the mountain in life, everything is going our way. However, there are those times in our life that our good fortune begins to slide, and we become stuck in the valley. That is the time that we need to look more closely at our life and see what we need to do to climb back on top. We should all be in the business of supporting others and helping them through the lows in life. We all need a little encouragement occasionally. Learn to become a good listener!

"But encourage one another daily as it is called 'Today', so that none of you may be hardened by sin's deceitfulness." (Heb. 3:13)

HELP THE WEAK:

Because you are strong, help those that are weak. We all have our own demons to deal with, but whether you realize it or not, you are stronger mentally, physically, and spiritually than many of those around you. Help does not always need to come in the form of money. You might be able to extend a helping hand to the elderly, or someone with a disability; or you may be able to offer a prayer or a comforting word to someone who has suffered a loss, be it loss of a family member, loss of a home, a shortage of food, etc. It may be helping with clean-up, supplying water and non-perishables, or even words of encouragement to those who have faced a natural disaster, i.e., hurricanes and tornadoes, floods, volcano, or an out-of-control fire. Help is always encouraged and appreciated in disasters such as these. And if you are able, financial assistance goes a long way in helping those in distress.

"To the weak, I became weak, to win the weak. I became all things to all people so that by all possible means I might save some." (1 Cor. 9:22)

BE PATIENT WITH EVERYONE:

Easier said than done, right? Wrong! If your heart is filled with a love and compassion for others, it will not be hard at all to develop a patience for others. Most often, we are in a hurry! We do not want to take the time to share our precious time with others. Matthew 13:9 says, "Whoever has ears let them hear." You will be encouraged to find that if you "listen" more to others, as opposed to talking about yourself, you may find that things are not as bad as you thought they were in your own life. You may even be able to offer some words of encouragement to lift them up.

"A person's wisdom yields patience; it is to one's glory to overlook an offense." (Pro.19:11)

MAKE SURE NOBODY PAYS BACK WRONG FOR WRONG:

Do you have that "get even" mentality? Assume that someone wrongs you. The first thing out of your mouth is, "I'll get even with them!" or "They're going to pay for that!" It is human nature to take the offensive and feel, in your mind, that the other party deserves whatever you feel is "even." But what if we were able to pause for a few seconds and consider the consequences because of our own actions? Actually, relationships have been destroyed due to a hasty decision. Friendships have been either won or lost due to a lack of self-control. A little patience coupled with wisdom and understanding can usually resolve most misunderstandings. We often display unnecessary anger and hatred toward others because we feel mistreated. Forgiveness is essential to resolving and maintaining a stressful relationship. A little tender "Love thy neighbor" never hurts either!

"Love is patient, love is kind. It does not envy, it does not boast, it is not proud. It does not dishonor others, it is not self-seeking, it is not easily angered, it keeps no record of wrongs." (1 Cor. 13:4-5)

ALWAYS STRIVE TO DO WHAT IS GOOD
FOR EACH OTHER AND EVERYONE ELSE:

Once again, if we practice patience, kindness, and thoughtfulness for others, we will find that an attitude of gratitude will go a long way in doing "what is good." Respect for others and for their property is a necessary part of living in this world with others; treating others the way that we expect to be treated. Lastly, be considerate and without fault. It has been said that you can catch more flies with honey than you can with vinegar although I have never tried!

"How good and pleasant it is when God's people live together in unity!" (Ps. 133:1)

REJOICE ALWAYS:

We should find boundless joy in our everyday life as a Christian just in knowing that we are alive and well and living under the lordship of our God. Troubles may be all around us, and problems may befall us; but we can take immense joy in knowing that God is always there to lift us up and protect us. We should exult Him and His holy name regardless of our circumstances. When we are weak, He is strong! Therefore, we should never allow fear or trembling to overtake us.

"Rejoice in the Lord always, I will say it again: Rejoice! Let your gentleness be evident to all. The Lord is near." (Php. 4:4)

Pray Continually:

We live in a hectic world! We find ourselves caught up in the hustle and bustle of everyday life to meet the demands of our ever-changing world. You may say, "I am so busy, how can I find time to pray?" That can be a very difficult question to answer. Sometimes we need to slow our life and our busy schedule down so that we *make* time to be with God in prayer. Everyone should be able to take a few minutes of quiet time to pray. We can give thanks to the Lord for bringing us through another day and asking for deliverance through the coming days ahead. We can also offer up prayers for family or a loved one, for those who are sick and afflicted, or for those who may be in distress due to an unforeseeable situation in their life. Pray for our nation, pray for our leaders, pray for our enemies. And finally, take time to give praise, honor, and glory to God. We can never find too much to pray about!

"Do not be anxious about anything, but in every situation, by prayer and petition, with thanksgiving present your requests to God. And the peace of God, which transcends all understanding, will guard your hearts and your minds in Christ Jesus." (Php.4:6-7)

Give thanks in all circumstances:

Have you ever faced a situation where you have hit rock bottom, you are out of options, and you feel so bad mentally that you cannot even muster up the strength to go to God in prayer? I am sure most of us have. And no matter how hard we may desire to take our situation to the Lord in prayer, our heart just is not in it. This verse *does* state that we should give thanks in *all* circumstances. We can thank God for the good *and* the bad that occurs in our life. Maybe if we were thanking God when things start to affect us negatively, we might not have to hit rock bottom before we decide to pray. Simply uttering a word of thanks during tough times is not only important to God but is good for our own well-being.

"Give thanks in all circumstances; for this is God's will for you in Christ Jesus." (1 Thes. 5:18)

Do not quench the Spirit:

To begin with, we may need to understand the meaning of "quench." The best way to explain this is by using the example of drinking water or a soft drink to "quench our thirst." Thus, we use the drink to extinguish or to overwhelm our thirst. The word "extinguish" can be related to a putting out a flame or fire; but we can also use the term figuratively to express our sensations and emotions. Similarly, how do we quench the Spirit? One such way is to treat a message with contempt that we discern is not valid or truthful by biblical standards, be it prophecy or the spoken or written word of another. By treating such a message with contempt, we are essentially rejecting it. We might even believe that a message did not come from the Spirit and choose to ignore it.

"Love not the world, neither the things that are in the world. If any man loves the world, the love of the Father is not in Him." (1 John 2:15)

Do not treat prophecies with contempt but test them all:

Assume that a prophecy was made, but we decide to reject it. Or we believe that the prophecy did not come from the Holy Spirit. We choose to ignore it when, in fact, the message was from God. We are treating such a prophecy with contempt. Therefore, we want to avoid "Blasphemy against the Holy Spirit" which is conscious and in hardened opposition to truth, "because the Spirit is Truth" (1 John 5:6). Conscious and hardened resistance to the truth leads us away from humility and repentance, and without repentance, there can be no forgiveness. That is why discernment is so important.

"Love never fails. But where there are prophecies, they will cease; where there are tongues, they will be stilled; where there is knowledge, it will pass away." (1Cor. 13:8-9)

Hold on to what is good:

As you grow in your Christian experience, continue to admonish others, lift them up, and you will be rewarded. Be willing and able to offer a little gentle, friendly advice and encourage one another. If done out of love and respect, you may be able to help someone else through circumstances which may not have ended well for them. Doing so only requires a couple of minutes of our time to help another human being avoid the trappings of life.

"Woe to those who call evil good and good evil, who put darkness for light and light for darkness, who put bitter for sweet and sweet for bitter." (Isa. 5:20)

Reject every kind of evil:

How do we rid ourselves of all manner of evil? The best way to rid ourselves of evil is to know what to look for. What are those personality traits that will perfect our being? There are seven virtues that we can develop for overcoming evil. Opposite the seven virtues, there are seven corresponding sins that stand in our way, thus causing us to falter. It is not hard to see the sharp contrast between the two.

Choose "Good" over "Evil":

1. <u>Humility</u> over <u>Pride</u> (Humbleness or modesty as opposed to deep pleasure derived from one's own achievement or self-gratification)
2. <u>Charity</u> over <u>Greed</u> (Generosity or unselfishness as opposed to covetousness or gluttonous)
3. <u>Chastity</u> over <u>Lust</u> (Refraining from extramarital or especially from all, sexual intercourse as opposed to adultery, which is a mortal sin, or intentional immoral thoughts)
4. <u>Gratitude</u> over <u>Envy</u> (Gratefulness or thankfulness as opposed to jealousy over the blessings and achievements of others)
5. <u>Temperance</u> over <u>Gluttony</u> (Moderation or self-restraint as opposed to over-indulgence or a lack of self-restraint in food, drink, wealth items especially as status tokens)
6. <u>Patience</u> over <u>Wrath</u> (Accepting or tolerating delays, trouble or suffering without getting upset as opposed to becoming angry or irritated)

7. <u>Diligence</u> over <u>Sloth</u> (Careful and persistent work or effort as opposed to avoidance of physical or spiritual work)

> "Love does not delight in evil but rejoices with the truth. It always protects, always trusts, always hopes, always perseveres." (1Cor. 13:6-7)

Something to Consider:

People often say, "It's your choice, choose wisely," without giving thought to its deeper meaning. The Bible tells us that fear of God leads to wisdom. And wisdom only comes from understanding by way of the knowledge that we gain through past experiences. So, when asked to "choose wisely," consider the meaning in the deeper context, and let God work out the details.

CHAPTER 5

HEAVENLY THOUGHTS AND DESIRES

"Since you have been raised with Christ, set your hearts on things above, where Christ is, seated at the right hand of God. Set your minds on things above, not on earthly things. For you died, and your life is now hidden with Christ in God."

COLOSSIANS 3:1-3

The following is taken from Colossians 3:5-15:

1. Put to death, whatever belongs to your earthly nature: sexual immorality, impurity, lust, evil desires, and greed, which is idolatry.
2. Rid yourselves of all such things as these: anger, rage, malice, slander, and filthy language from your lips.

3. Do not lie to each other, since you have taken off your old self with its practices and have put on the new self, which is being renewed in knowledge in the image of its Creator.

4. Clothe yourselves with compassion, kindness, humility, gentleness, and patience.

5. Bear with each other and forgive one another if any of you has a grievance against someone.

6. Forgive as the Lord forgave you.

7. And over all these virtues put on love, which binds them all together in perfect unity.

8. Let the peace of Christ rule in your hearts, since as members of one body you were called to peace. And be thankful.

How do we "Put to death" that which belongs to our earthly nature? We begin by "casting out" or removing those things that hinder our growth spiritually. Anything that is not of God is sin. But how do we know that? Because the Bible makes it very clear the kind of behavior that He expects of us. In fact, we should consider all things that take precedence or come between our relationship with God. We take for granted our labor for riches and fame. Our love for money, our homes, and any other possession that we love more than God can lead us to idolatry if it supersedes our relationship with God. And how often do we idolize famous actors, musicians, sports professionals, and the like?

Previously, we mentioned those traits and characteristics that are unbecoming of the person renewed in knowledge and in the image of the Creator. Anger, rage, malice, slander, filthy language, and lies have no place in the life of he who has cloaked himself in the Masters' image. Instead, we should clothe ourselves in those traits that display the fruit of the Spirit in us. Be willing to forgive others as the Lord has forgiven you, because complete forgiveness of others leads to purity in our own heart.

Therefore, love others, for it is written, "Love the Lord your God with all your heart and with all your soul and with all your mind. This is the first and greatest commandment. And the second is like it: 'Love your neighbor as yourself.' All the Law and the Prophets hang on these two commandments" (Matt. 22:37-40). If you can love others, regardless of skin color (red, yellow, black, or white), large or small in stature, strong or weak, rich or poor, disabled, those full of love or those who are hateful and lacking in compassion…if you can find it in your heart to love *all* people, then you have fulfilled the Great Commandment. Consider this: we were all endowed by our Creator who gave us life and breath. We are human beings, and we are not inherently different. If we allow the peace of Christ to rule in our heart, how can we not be at peace with others?

> "Search me, God, and know my heart; test me and know my anxious thoughts. See if there is any offensive way in me and lead me in the way everlasting." (Ps. 139:23-24)

Something to Consider:

Gold is refined and purified by using hydrochloric acid and nitric acid to dissolve the impurities. Likewise, God gives us the indwelling Holy Spirit to help us separate the impurities in our life. The Holy Spirit helps to refine us like pure gold so that we might be filled with the fruit of the Spirit.

CHAPTER 6

FACING TRIALS AND PERSECUTIONS

**"Consider it pure joy, my brothers and sisters, whenever
you face trials of many kinds, because you know
that the testing of your faith produces perseverance.
Let perseverance finish its work so that you may be
mature and complete, not lacking anything."**

JAMES 1:2-4

Trials and persecution can bring unexpected challenges into our life that we never have dreamed of. We are overcome with addictions, petty crimes, relationships with others that have become a disappointment. We may try every possible means to correct the situation, or make amends, but things continue to go awry. Maybe we have even tried to effectively use some of the methods listed previously. In 2 Corinthians 4:8-9, we find that our situation may be futile, *but*:

- We are hard pressed on every side, *but* not crushed.
- Perplexed, *but* not in despair.
- Persecuted, *but* not abandoned.
- Struck down, *but* not destroyed.

As I mentioned, we may face many blows in life. We may become disappointed, frustrated, dismayed. We may feel like we are pounded from every side like a boxer in the ring. We may feel like we are down for the count. We may feel perplexed, but we still have that inner will to fight back. We may feel persecuted, but never abandoned so long as God is in our corner. We may feel struck down, but we are not out. Remember: a winner never quits, and a quitter never wins! Believe in yourself and accept in your heart that you can face the consequences head on so long as God is your navigator.

> "Bless those who persecute you; bless and do not curse. Rejoice with those who rejoice; mourn with those who mourn. Live in harmony with one another. Do not be proud but be willing to associate with people of low position. Do not be conceited." (Rom. 12:14-16)

Something to Consider:

We often say, "Put your best foot forward." Conversely, we sometimes feel like we are taking one step forward and two steps back. It is difficult to put your best foot forward when you are stuck in a rut. Stay positive! Stay focused! Things *will* change! Regardless of the situation, God says, "I will not leave you or forsake you." Perhaps He is testing your faith in Him so that He can provide a greater blessing.

CHAPTER 7

THE VIRTUE OF PATIENCE

"May you live a life worthy of the Lord and please Him in every way: bearing fruit in every good work, growing in the knowledge of God, being strengthened with all power according to His glorious might so that you may have great endurance and patience, and giving joyful thanks to the Father..."

COLOSSIANS 1:12

From receiving an answer to our prayers, right down to every individual daily chore in our life, we need to learn to be patient. It is not easy when we are constantly on the go, rushing to appointments, striving to meet deadlines, getting the kids to a ballgame, etc. It is funny that when we need to be somewhere on time or accomplish something that demands our attention at that very instant, we always seem to run into delays and unforeseen circumstances. We feel like we will never reach our destination.

Let the following characteristics help you to develop patience in your life. You will find that your day will not only be less stressful, but your time will be more enjoyable (assuming you allow for a little unexpected disruption along the way). And chances are, you will still probably manage to accomplish everything on your list.

<u>What are the characteristics of a patient person?</u> (Taken from James 5:7-12)

1. Be patient and stand firm like the farmer who waits for the land to yield its valuable crops, patiently waiting for the autumn and spring rains.
2. Do not grumble against one another or you will be judged. The judge is standing at the door.
3. We count as blessed those who persevere. The Lord is full of compassion and mercy.
4. Do not swear, not by heaven or by earth or by anything else. All you need to say is simply "yes" or "no." Otherwise, you will be condemned.

<u>Consider how prayer is essential in a patient persons' life</u>: (Taken from James 5:13-16)

1. Is anyone among you in trouble? Let them pray.
2. Is anyone happy? Let them sing songs of praise.
3. Is anyone among you sick? Let them call the elders of the church to pray over them and anoint them with oil in the name of the Lord. The prayer offered

in faith will make the person well. The Lord will raise them up.

4. Confess your sins to each other and pray for each other so that you may be healed. The prayer of a righteous person is powerful and effective.

"Do not be anxious about anything, but in every situation, by prayer and petition, with thanksgiving, present your requests to God. And the peace of God which transcends all understanding, will guard your hearts and your minds in Christ Jesus" (Phi. 4:6-7).

SOMETHING TO CONSIDER:

Trials and misfortune are nothing more than an experience to teach us how to cope. We can only grow from these experiences if we seek God, have patience, and understand where those trials and misfortunes are coming from.

CHAPTER 8

THE IMPORTANCE OF CONTROLLING THE TONGUE

"For by your words, you will be acquitted and by your words you will be condemned."

MATTHEW 12:47

When we put bits into the mouths of horses to make them obey us, we can turn the whole animal (Taken from James 3:3-10):

1. Likewise, the tongue is a small part of the body, but it makes great boasts.
2. Consider what a great forest is set on fire by a small spark. The tongue is also a fire, a world of evil among the parts of the body. It corrupts the whole

body, sets the whole course of one's life on fire, and is itself set on fire by hell.

3. All kinds of animals, birds, reptiles, and sea creatures are being tamed and have been tamed by humankind, but no human being can tame the tongue. It is a restless evil, full of deadly poison.

4. With the tongue we praise our Lord and Father, and with it we curse human beings, who have been made in God's likeness. Out of the same mouth come praise and cursing.

How can one part of the body be so evil and yet so uplifting? The tongue can spue out curses and obscenities on the one hand, and offer praise, compliments, and worship on the other.

We may boast and brag to make ourselves look good to others, or we may believe that we are important; but how often does our own intentions make us look small in eyes of others?

Whether our thoughts are pure or impure in nature, those thoughts all arise from our mind, i.e., what we think and what we feel. Our thoughts can be kind and thoughtful, loving, joyful, excitable; or they can be harmful, hurtful, ugly, abrasive, and thoughtless. The tongue is so powerful that our words can bring down the strong and the mighty. Lies and rumors can lead to conversations that can ruin the reputation of those who either meant well or have done nothing wrong at all. Peaceful protests can quickly spiral out of control simply by one or more instigators inciting a crowd to riot. However, it is important to understand that all words begin as thought! How you control those thoughts is up to you.

Sometimes in our haste, it is easy to be misunderstood when we speak. We may respond by saying something rude or obnoxious. Or we reply with anger in our voice. Our speech may have been taken out of context, but once uttered, those words said in a moment of high emotion, are hard to take back. Friendships can easily be won or lost based on how we answer others. The Bible tells us that the sinners' mouth is "full of curses and bitterness" (Rom. 3:14), while the believer's mouth is opened to praise and glorify God (Rom. 15:6). Unfortunately, words are used to stir crowds to worship on one extreme or to stir riotous behavior on the other. So, as you can see, our words can create strong emotion. We can either be a source to lift others up, or a voice to tear others down. It is up to you to decide. A good rule of thumb is to pause and think before inserting "foot in mouth."

> "The words of the reckless pierce like swords,
> but the tongue of the wise brings healing.
> Truthful lips endure forever, but a lying tongue
> lasts only a moment." (Pro 12:18-19)

Something to Consider:

Most of us are prone to gossip. Our conversation is "He/she said;" or "he/she did this or that;" Or "did you see what so and so did?" It is easy to talk about others or bring them down. The Bible tells us that the tongue is sharper than a two-edged sword; that we should control our tongue, and that our answers should be "yeh or nay."

Our words can be sarcastic, or even caustic, if we are speaking directly to others. The next time we start to gossip, we should pause and ask the Father to provide a kinder, softer word to our speech in such a way that we do not offend or persecute others.

CHAPTER 9

THE IMPORTANCE OF WISDOM

"Who is wise and understanding among you? Let
them show it by their good life, by deeds done
in the humility that comes from wisdom."

JAMES 3:13

How do we know whether wisdom is important if we do
not understand what wisdom truly is? If you answered that
wisdom is knowledge, you are correct, for wisdom is defined
as the quality of having experience, knowledge, and good
judgment. In other words, it is the quality of being wise. So,
what is knowledge? Knowledge is facts, information, and
skills acquired by a person through experience or education.
Wisdom is based upon knowledge. We can be wise and
knowledgeable, but we cannot be wise without knowledge.

In other words, Knowledge is knowing what to say, and wisdom is knowing when to say it.

Much can be said about the diverse types of wisdom. Some sources mention two distinct types, while others mention as many as seven. The three types of wisdom most often referred to are human or earthly wisdom which is wisdom derived from our own knowledge and experiences; demonic wisdom which is from Satan, the ruler of this world; and Godly wisdom which is spiritually discerning and Godly spiritual. We can get a better understanding here as to how Godly wisdom is at work in our lives.

The following verses taken from Proverbs 4:23-27 tell us how to protect our heart, our mouth, our eyes, and our feet:

1. Above all else, guard your <u>heart</u>, for everything you do flows from it.
2. Keep your <u>mouth</u> free of perversity; keep corrupt talk far from your lips.
3. Let your <u>eyes</u> look straight ahead; fix your gaze directly before you.
4. Give careful thought to the paths for your <u>feet</u> and be steadfast in all your ways.
5. Do not turn to the right or the left; <u>keep your foot from evil</u>. (Pro. 4:23-27)

"Get wisdom, get understanding; do not forget my words or turn away from them. Do not forget wisdom, and she will protect you; love her, and she will watch over you. The beginning of wisdom is this: Get wisdom. Though it cost all you have, get understanding" (Pro. 4:5-7).

The following verses found in Proverbs 3:27-31 will help us to understand what not to do:

1. Do not withhold good from those to whom it is due, when it is in your power to act.
2. Do not say to your neighbor, "Come back tomorrow and I'll give it to you" when you already have it with you.
3. Do not plot harm against your neighbor, who lives trustfully near you.
4. Do not accuse anyone for no reason when they have done you no harm.
5. Do not envy the violent or choose any of their ways.

"But if you harbor bitter envy and selfish ambition in your hearts, do not boast about it or deny the truth. Such "Wisdom" does not come down from heaven is earthly, unspiritual, and demonic; and earthly wisdom harbors bitter envy, chases selfish ambition, and is boastful and denies the truth. Where there is envy and selfish ambition, there is disorder and every evil practice." (Jas. 3:15-16)

How do we discern earthly wisdom from heavenly Wisdom? Let us examine those characteristics that come from heaven. (taken from James 3:17-18)

- It is pure,
- Peace-loving,
- Considerate,
- Submissive,
- Full of mercy and good fruit,

- Impartial and Sincere.
- Peacemakers who sow in peace, reap a harvest of righteousness.

> "Submit yourselves, then, to God. Resist the devil, and he will flee from you. Come near to God, and He will come near to you. Wash your hands, you sinners, and purify your hearts, you double-minded." (Jas. 4:7-8)

Something to Consider:

Spiritual growth requires planting your feet firmly on solid ground, i.e. grounded in the Bible and God's word; nurtured by the Holy Spirit who provides discernment in all things; all things; and life...because Jesus said, "I am the way, the truth, and the life. No one comes to the Father except through me." (John 14:6) "Let your light shine before others, that they may see your good deeds and glorify your Father in heaven." (John 5:16)

CHAPTER 10

CHRISTIAN OBEDIENCE TO GOVERNMENT

"Let everyone be subject to the governing authorities, for there is no authority except that which God has established. The authorities that exist have been established by God."

ROMANS 13:1

Do you want to be free of fear of the one in authority? The Bible tells us that "The authorities that exist have been established by God. Consequently, whoever rebels against the authority is rebelling against what God has instituted, and those who do so will bring judgment on themselves," God's words, not mine! (Rom. 13:1-2). Consider the following taken from Romans 13:3-14:

1. Do what is right and you will be commended.
2. It is necessary to submit to the authorities, not only because of possible punishment, but also as a matter of conscience.
3. If you owe taxes, pay taxes; if revenue, then revenue; if respect, then respect; if honor, then honor.
4. Let no debt remain outstanding, except the continuing debt to love one another, for whoever loves others has fulfilled the law.
5. Love your neighbor as yourself.
6. Put aside the deeds of darkness and put on the armor of light.
7. Behave decently, as in the daytime, not in carousing and drunkenness, not in sexual immorality and debauchery, not in dissension and jealousy.
8. Clothe yourselves with the Lord Jesus Christ, and do not think about how to gratify the desires of the flesh.

Obeying the laws of government are not any different than obeying God's law. Laws have consequences! When we fail to obey those laws, we must answer to those in authority. Unfortunately, we are living in an age where many believe they are above the law. It is not hard to find examples of this. Speed limits are simply ignored because of our fast-paced world. Instead of driving a couple of miles per hour over the speed limit, we drive 10-20 mph over the posted speed. Oftentimes, we speed through residential districts or school zones without any thought of unavoidable mishaps. And what about minor traffic infractions such as failure to use a turn signal, driving without insurance, driving under the influence? Decent law-abiding citizens seldom commit crimes which are not only punishable by man's laws but are punishable by God's laws as well. These include harder crimes which include murder, rape, robbery, defacing property, breaking and entering, tax evasion. These and other similar crimes are not characteristic of a Godly person.

I could talk about the subject of bankruptcy, government programs such as food stamps and unemployment benefits. Those programs that were designed to help the poor, the needy, and the unemployed are quite often abused by those who feel "entitled" or are too lazy to earn an income for that which they desire.

When is enough, enough? Can we ever satisfy our insatiable wants and desires? We can! By heeding God's word and living a fruitful life…a life of peace, love, and joy. We can fulfill God's law by loving one another and always showing respect to others where respect is due. If we live according to God's laws, we will be more likely to observe and obey man's laws; and we will reap His rewards.

We are told to put aside the deeds of darkness and behave as we would in the light. How? By putting on the armor of light. If we can clothe ourselves with the Lord Jesus Christ, and we do not think of ways to gratify the flesh, we can become Children of the Light, living in purity and righteousness. We can still have the desires of our heart, but they truly begin to come to us as blessings from our Father in Heaven.

"Those who live according to the flesh have their minds set on what the flesh desires; but those who live in accordance with the Spirit have their minds set on what the Spirit desires. The mind governed by the flesh is death, but the mind governed by the Spirit is life and peace. The mind governed by the flesh is hostile to God; it does not submit to God's law, nor can it do so. Those who are in the realm of the flesh cannot please God." (Rom. 8:5-8)

SOMETHING TO CONSIDER:

Throughout life, we are in a tug of war between God and Satan with us stuck in the middle. God calls us to right our lives and do good. At the same time, Satan is pulling in the opposite direction to have fun and enjoy the pleasures of life. God offers salvation and eternal life through His love for each of us, while Satan offers instant gratification and eternal damnation when we reach our expiration date. We do have a choice. This worldly life is only temporary!

CHAPTER 11

GIVE PRAISE TO THE LORD

"Praise the Lord my soul; all my inmost being, praise His Holy name. Praise the Lord, my soul, and forget not all His benefits."

PSALMS 103:1-2

And what are the benefits that the Lord bestows on each of us? Let us peruse this subject, taken from Psalm 103:3-12:

1. He forgives all our sins and heals all our diseases.
2. He redeems our life from the pit, and crowns us with love and compassion.
3. He satisfies our desires with good things.
4. He works righteousness and justice for all the oppressed.
5. The Lord is gracious and compassionate.

6. He is slow to anger, abounding in love.
7. He will not always accuse, nor will He harbor His anger forever.
8. He does not treat us as our sins deserve or repay us according to our iniquities.
9. For as high as the heavens are above the earth, so great is His love for those who fear Him.
10. As far as the east is from the west, so far has He removed our transgressions from us.

"The Lord has established His throne in heaven, and His kingdom rules over all." (Ps. 103:19)

The list above tells us that our God deserves our honor, glory, and praise for all that He has done and continues to do for each of us. He has shown us His love and compassion. Because of His forgiving nature, He is always willing to forgive those who have sinned and fallen away. God's word tells us that He will forgive us seventy times seven. And I know from experience that He will start over again at 491 if that is what it takes to get our attention. So that tells us that He does not hold His anger against us forever. He is righteous and just. God does not play favorites! He treats each of us equally. He is omnipotent, omniscient, and omnipresent (all powerful, all knowing, and ever present). He will never forsake us if we are truthful, honest, and open to doing His will and obeying His commands. He is all that and much more. And all He asks of us is that we do His will. I call it the SOW Principle: Serve, Obey, and Witness!

Why should we not live our life out of respect for who He is. The trade-off: freedom from our earthly habits and desires for eternal life, born again as a new creation in Jesus Christ! Glory to His Holy Name!

> "But from everlasting to everlasting the Lord's love is with those who fear Him, and His righteousness with their children's children… with those who keep His covenant and remember to obey His precepts." Ps. 103:17-18

SOMETHING TO CONSIDER:

A God who has authority over His spiritual beings and mortal man, and has control over our destiny, is to be served and worshiped with respect without question of His universal purpose for our life.

CHAPTER 12

SIN VERSUS BEARING FRUIT

"Walk by the Spirit, and you will not gratify the
desires of the flesh. For the flesh desires what
is contrary to the Spirit, and the Spirit what is
contrary to the flesh. They conflict with each other,
so that you are not to do whatever you want."

GALATIANS 5:16-17

ACTS OF A SINFUL NATURE:

"The acts of the flesh are obvious: sexual immorality,
impurity and debauchery, idolatry and witchcraft, hatred,
discord, jealousy, fits of rage, selfish ambition, dissension,
factions and envy, drunkenness, orgies, and the like" (Gal.
5:19-21).

FRUIT OF THE SPIRIT:

"But the fruit of the Spirit is love, joy, peace, forbearance, kindness, goodness, faithfulness, gentleness, and self-control. Against such things there is no law. Those who belong to Christ Jesus have crucified the flesh with its passions and desires. Since we live by the Spirit, let us keep in step with the Spirit" (Gal. 5:22-25).

By now, you should begin to see how the acts of your sinful nature can be in direct conflict with living a holy life. It should be easier for you to identify the characteristics of the sinner vs. the righteous. And you should be able to understand where you stand. If you identify with the sinner, do not allow those feelings of emptiness or despair to bring you down. There is hope! Put on the armor of God! Open your eyes so that you may see more clearly what you must change in your life, how you might change your path, and begin to walk closer to God.

I agree, that is easier said than done! I know because I faced the same dilemma. But with persistence, your path will become clearer, and your walk will be rewarding in ways you cannot imagine. Patience is a virtue! Suffice to say, any change takes time. The old sayings apply here: "anything worth doing is worth doing right; you will not see a change overnight; and anything good is worth the wait!"

"If someone is caught in a sin, you who live by the Spirit should restore that person gently. But watch yourselves, or you also may be tempted. Carry each other's burdens, and in this way, you will fulfill the law of Christ. If anyone thinks they are something when they are not, they deceive themselves. Each one should test their own actions. Then they can take pride in themselves alone, without comparing themselves to someone else, for each one should carry their own load" (Gal. 6:2-4).

Hell is full of those who have ignored God's word, who have been content to live lavish lifestyles, who enjoy the fruits of their labor, enjoying the pleasures of darkness. But God says, "I will put an end to your greed, your lust, your pride, and you will know that I am the Lord your God." Sin seeks to steal God's glory to satisfy the sinner. Exodus 20:4-5 tells us that if we serve idols or worship any other gods, He will punish us, our children, our grandchildren and even our great grandchildren. Therefore, it is said, "Do not conform to the pattern of this world but be transformed by the renewing of your mind" (Rom. 12:2). Leave the patterns of corruption and evil in this life to those who are conformed to this life (those who love the world) as you pursue a Godly way of life.

> "Let the message of Christ dwell among you richly as you teach and admonish one another with all wisdom through psalms, hymns, and songs from the Spirit, singing to God with gratitude in your hearts. And whatever you do, whether in word or deed, do it all in the name of the Lord Jesus, giving thanks to God the Father through Him." (Col. 3:16-17)

SOMETHING TO CONSIDER:

Sin has no boundaries! That is why God has given us the Ten Commandments to live by (See Appendix). We can set parameters by which we will not allow sin to enter in.

Help us Father to see You more clearly, and to love You more deeply so that we might grow in the likeness of your Son.

CHAPTER 13

SIN IN THE LAST DAYS

"For the time will come when people will not put up with
sound doctrine. Instead, to suit their own desires, they
will gather around them a great number of teachers to
say what their itching ears want to hear. They will turn
their ears away from the truth and turn aside to myths."

2 TIMOTHY 4:3-4

But mark this: There will be terrible times in the last days
(2 Tim. 3:1-5):

1. People will be lovers of themselves- self-indulged
   (name-brand products and clothing, cell phones,
   video games are examples).
2. Lovers of money- greedy; obsessed with money
   more than anything else in life.
3. Boastful, proud, abusive- cocky, selfish, unforgiving.

4. Disobedient to their parents- disrespectful, uncompromising, threatening.

5. Ungrateful, unholy, without love- finding no joy in life; non-sympathetic, ungrateful for anything done on their behalf.

6. Unforgiving, slanderous- hateful, spiteful, unwilling to make amends.

7. Without self-control- lacking in self-restraint.

8. Brutal, not lovers of the good- shows no concern for life, property, or the feelings of others; such a person is simply evil.

9. Treacherous, rash, conceited- full of themselves, cannot be trusted, quick to judge others.

10. Lovers of pleasure rather than lovers of God-does not have time for God; would rather enjoy life today than worry about eternity.

11. Having a form of godliness but denying its power-those who show all manner of godliness in their emotions and actions but lack the love of God in their heart.

Have nothing to do with such people!

There are Six Things the Lord Hates, Seven That are Detestable to Him (Pro. 6:16-19):

1. Haughty eyes: Someone who is blatantly and disdainfully proud; arrogant; having or showing an attitude of superiority and contempt for people or things perceived to be inferior.

2. A lying tongue: A lie is a lie is a lie, no matter how great or small. Even a "little white lie" is still a lie.

3. Hands that shed innocent blood: This could be anyone who is involved in a shooting, stabbing, poisoning or any other act to kill or maim another who is blameless or guilt-free, i.e., one of the Ten Commandments.

4. A heart that devises wicked schemes: Wicked schemes go beyond mere pranks. We defined "wicked" earlier as someone who is evil or morally wrong. Their thoughts might even be said to be ungodly, unrighteous, or unholy. Anything from petty theft to unspeakable acts of horror would fall into this category.

5. Feet that are quick to rush into evil:
Our personal sins such as drinking, drugs, sex and pornography, smoking, etc. (any demon that controls our mind and our thoughts to the extent that we feel like we <u>can't</u> give it up, or <u>won't</u>, due to the pleasure that is derived from the act).

6. A false witness who pours out lies: A false witness is one who twists reality, makes up stories, or shames others.

7. A person who stirs up conflict in the community: Consider the person who spreads rumors or likes to spread gossip about others. They might serve in a social or political role which they believe gives them a platform to voice their opinions about problems that concern them specifically.

"<u>Disaster will overtake those in an instant who are disobedient</u>" (Taken from Pr. 6:12-15):

- A troublemaker and a villain who goes about with a corrupt mouth.
- One who winks maliciously with his eye.
- He who signals with his feet and motions with his fingers.
- He who plots evil in his heart. He always stirs up conflict.

> "The fear of the Lord is the beginning of wisdom, and knowledge of the Holy One is understanding." (Pro. 9:10)

SOMETHING TO CONSIDER:

We live in a world full of sin and sinners. Sin is a lack of self-discipline, a lack of self-control, and a lack of desire to do God's will in our lives. God gives us "free will" to do what *we* want without limitations: but service to the Father asks us to establish parameters regarding our faith. Stepping out of bounds is *never* pleasing to God.

I have saved the chapter on Salvation for last. For those of you who may not have been saved, or for those who seek to be saved, turn the page. Your Salvation awaits!

CHAPTER 14

PRAY FOR CONTINUED SALVATION

**"The Lord is my Light and my salvation;
whom shall I fear? The Lord is the stronghold
of my life; of whom shall I be afraid?"**

PSALM 27:1

Asking God for salvation daily (Ps. 119:129-136):

1. Your statutes are wonderful; therefore, I obey them.
2. The unfolding of your words gives light; it gives understanding to the simple.
3. I open my mouth and pant, longing for your command.
4. Turn to me and have mercy on me, as you always do to those who love your name.

5. Direct my footsteps according to your word, let no sin rule over me.
6. Redeem me from human oppression that I may obey your precepts.
7. Make your face shine on your servant and teach me your decrees.
8. Streams of tears flow from my eyes, for your law is not obeyed.

What exactly is salvation? It is God's grace! To gain a broader understanding of salvation, it may also be defined as deliverance or redemption of the soul from sin and its consequences which brings us into a relationship with God through Jesus Christ. 1 John 1:9 tells us that, "If we confess our sins, He who is faithful and just will forgive us our sins and cleanse us from all unrighteousness." In other words, we must first recognize our sinful nature before God and ask that He forgive us for our wrongdoing. We know that God is faithful, and He is just. And because He is full of mercy and love for us, He forgives us of our sins, and cleanses us from all our iniquities. Even though we are undeserving of this act of unreserved love and forgiveness, He wipes the slate clean and offers us a new life through His Son, Jesus Christ. It is a gift of freedom made possible by the death of Jesus on the Cross who bore the sins of the world forever so that we might have eternal life. No greater love has ever been displayed than this: that Jesus laid down His life for all humanity.

Expect your life to change! You are now a new creation, born again as a Child of God. You may experience a change in the way you feel and/or in the way you act. The change may be gradual, or you may find that you have changed significantly. You may encounter roadblocks that you never expected, but do not give up. This is oftentimes normal for the new believer because Satan does not want you to change. But you have the Armor of God to protect you. Read your Bible, attend a church which teaches the true word of God, and pray continually. Remember what you have learned here and memorize verses to help you grow. Growth is important! If you are not growing, you can become stagnant; and stagnation can reopen the door to temptation. Rely on your faith and trust in The Holy One to do what He has promised to do. So, what is next you ask?

We are saved to carry out the work for which God has placed us on earth. And that is to be the hands and feet of Jesus Christ so that we can go forth and share the good news of the Gospel with others by displaying God's love through our actions. Receiving salvation is not the end of the process. In fact, it is just the beginning of a life-long process of continually being shaped into the person that God wants us to be. This means becoming more Christ-like. And we do this in grateful thanksgiving for the new life He has blessed us with. As we become more like Christ, God works through us to share Christ's love and grace with the world.

You may have already been saved, but you feel that you are still a sinner and may have to be baptized or saved again. I have struggled with the same dilemma. We are told that once you are saved, you are saved forever. Unfortunately, that never sank in. I was sprinkled as a Methodist and immersed when my wife and I were attending the Church of Christ.

But, as I mentioned in the introduction, salvation, for me, was not complete until I experienced God's mercy come upon me during the viewing of the <u>Passion of the Christ</u>. What I did not realize is that once we have been saved, we are redeemed for life. To believe anything less, is an insult to Jesus Christ, who forgave us of our sins upon redemption. If you have strayed, as sheep often do, you must find a way to return to the fold and say, "Forgive me Lord, for I have sinned;" and because our God is a merciful God, He will rescue you! Any time you feel low, confused, or stressed, remember what Jesus endured on the cross. He suffered for our redemption…and for our eternal life. Rejoice!

> "For the grace of God has appeared that offers salvation to all people. It teaches us to say 'No' to ungodliness and worldly passions, and to live self-controlled, upright and godly lives in this present age, while we wait for the blessed hope—the appearing of our great God and Savior, Jesus Christ, who gave himself for us to redeem us from all wickedness and to purify for Himself a people that are His very own, eager to do what is good" (Titus 2:11-14).

PRAYER FOR SALVATION:

Heavenly Father, I realize that I am a sinner and have broken Your laws. I understand that my sin has separated me from You. I am sorry and I ask You to forgive me. I accept the fact that Your Son Jesus Christ died for me, was resurrected, and is alive today and hears my prayers. I now open my heart's door and invite Jesus in to become

my Lord and my Savior. I give Him control and ask that He would rule and reign in my heart so that His perfect will would be accomplished in my life. In Jesus' name I pray. Amen.

SOMETHING TO CONSIDER:

Salvation does not give us a license to sin. Even though we are told that we are forgiven once we are saved, salvation does not give us a right to do as we please. For, by faith, we are no longer under man's law; we are now under God's law. We should develop the self-control needed to avoid sin so that we do not have to seek God's forgiveness every time we become weak.

FINAL THOUGHTS

Many are already lost in the world and enjoy their lifestyle. Quite frankly, they refuse to change. But for those with addictions (alcohol, drugs, sex and pornography, greed, gluttony), there are agencies and workers who are trained to help; for feelings of demonic possession, there are pastors and priests willing to assist you; for those who have an incurable disease or illness, pray for a cure. Open your eyes, search your heart, find those who will listen. Ask God to come into your life. And if you are willing, and you have the power within you to believe, it shall be done!

After all that has been said, you may think that I must be "Mr. Perfect." Contrary to that belief, nothing could be further from the truth. I have struggled with my own demons and battled life daily like everyone else. Admittedly, I <u>do not</u> live up to every word that I have written herein. However, I <u>strive daily</u> to live according to God's will for my life and do all that I can to become a better human being. None of us are perfect! We do not even come close to living a righteous life. But what we *are* expected to do is follow our perfect example (Jesus Christ) and allow Him to work in our lives and to live in our hearts. Only then are we made perfect in His love. May God bless you and keep you!

If you have been moved in any way to seek Jesus Christ in your life, please feel free to write me at the address below regarding your experience. I would love to hear from you and share your story of encouragement.

William Summers
138 Bogus Rd. SE
Washington Court House
Ohio 43128

questadgroup@yahoo.com

GLOSSARY
WORDS TO BECOME FAMILIAR WITH:

Biblical Terminology to Help Better Understand God's Word: The following list of words helps us to better understand the steps taken toward our salvation:

Admonitions- instruction, recommendation, guidance, direction.

Edification- to instruct and improve especially in moral and religious knowledge.

Justification- being declared righteous.

Reconciliation- a change in the relationship between God and man or man and man.

Redemption- the work of Christ on our behalf, whereby He purchases us, He ransoms us, at the price of His own life, securing our deliverance from the bondage and condemnation of sin.

Salvation- God's grace! It is the gift of freedom from our sins that Jesus made possible by taking the punishment for our sins on the cross.

Sanctification- growing in righteousness.

Additional words to help us better understand Biblical language:

Abhor- to reject, despise, deny, loath, hate.

Apostasy- the rejection of Christ by one who has been a Christian; also, an act of refusing to continue to follow, obey, or recognize a religious faith.

Discernment- the ability to choose between what is true and right and what is false and wrong; to discern something is to recognize its true validity (sin vs. godliness).

Extol- to glorify, exalt, to praise highly.

Grace- undeserved favor. Grace cannot be earned; it is something that is freely given.

Mercy- forgiveness or withholding punishment (the fruit of compassion).

Reverence- profound respect and love; a feeling of deep respect or awe; our admiration for Deity.

Sovereign- supreme, absolute, master, exalted.

Supplication- to plead humbly, a prayer asking for God's help.

It is important to know that our God is:

Omniscient- having complete or unlimited knowledge and understanding. He perceives all things.

Omnipotent- almighty; having unlimited authority or influence.

Omnipresent- God is always present in all places.

APPENDIX A
THE LORD'S PRAYER

Matthew 6:5-9 tells us how we should pray (taken from The King James version of The Holy Bible):

"And when thou prayest, thou shalt not be as the hypocrites are: for they love to pray standing in the synagogues and in the corners of the streets, that they may be seen of men. Verily I say unto you, they have their reward. But thou, when thou prayest, enter into thy closet, and when thou hast shut thy door, pray to thy Father which is in secret; and thy Father which seeth in secret shall reward thee openly. But when ye pray, use not vain repetitions, as the heathen do: for they think that they shall be heard for their much speaking. Be not ye therefore like unto them: for your Father knoweth what things ye have need of, before ye ask Him. After this manner therefore pray ye":

THE LORD'S PRAYER:

"Our Father which art in Heaven, Hallowed be thy name. Thy kingdom come, thy will be done in earth, as it is in heaven. Give us this day our daily bread. And forgive us our debts, as we forgive our debtors. And lead us not into temptation but deliver us from evil: For thine is the kingdom, and the power, and the glory, forever. Amen" (Matt. 6:9-13).

> "But if ye forgive men their trespasses, your heavenly Father will also forgive you: But if ye forgive not men their trespasses, neither will your Father forgive your trespasses." (Matt. 6:14-15)

APPENDIX B

THE APOSTLES CREED

I believe in God the Father Almighty, Maker of heaven and earth: and in Jesus Christ His only Son, our Lord; who was conceived by the Holy Ghost, born of the Virgin Mary, suffered under Pontius Pilate, was crucified, dead, and buried; He descended into hell; the third day He rose again from the dead; He ascended into heaven, and sitteth on the right hand of God the Father Almighty; from thence He shall come to judge the quick and the dead. I believe in the Holy Ghost; the holy Catholic Church; the communion of saints; the forgiveness of sins; the resurrection of the body; and the life everlasting. Amen! (KJV)

APPENDIX C
THE TEN COMMANDMENTS

The Ten Commandments may be found in Exodus 20:1-17 (KJV):

God spake all these words, saying, I am the Lord thy God, which have brought thee out of the land of Egypt, out of the house of bondage.

I.   Thou shalt have no other gods before me.

II.   Thou shalt not make unto thee any graven image, or any likeness of anything that is in heaven above, or that is in the earth beneath, or that is in the water under the earth: thou shalt not bow down thyself to them, nor serve them: for I the Lord thy God am a jealous God, visiting the iniquity of the fathers upon the children unto the third and fourth generation of them that hate me;

and showing mercy unto thousands of them that love me, and keep my commandments.

III. Thou shalt not take the name of the Lord thy God in vain; for the Lord will not hold him guiltless that taketh His name in vain.

IV. Remember the Sabbath day, to keep it holy. Six days shalt thou labor, and do all thy work: but the seventh day is the Sabbath of the Lord thy God: in it thou shalt not do any work, thou, nor thy son, not thy daughter, thy man-servant, nor thy maid-servant, nor thy cattle, nor thy stranger that is within thy gates: for in six days the Lord made heaven and earth, the sea, and all that in them is, and rested the seventh day: wherefore the Lord blessed the Sabbath day, and hallowed it.

V. Honor thy father and thy mother: that thy days may be long upon the land which the Lord thy God giveth thee.

VI. Thou shalt not kill.

VII. Thou shalt not commit adultery.

VIII. Thou shalt not steal.

IX. Thou shalt not bear false witness against thy neighbor.

X. Thou shalt not covet thy neighbor's house, thou shalt not covet thy neighbor's wife, nor his man-servant, nor his maid-servant, nor his ox, nor his ass, nor any thing that is thy neighbor's.

APPENDIX D

THE STORY BEHIND THE SONG: 'IT IS NO SECRET'

To contact Lindsay Terry, email lindsay976@earthlink.net.

If I asked you, "Do you know Stuart Hamblen?" you might pause for a few seconds. If I added that he had a "star" on Hollywood's Walk of Fame, placed there in 1978, then you might say, "Yes, Carl "Stuart" Hamblen, radio personality, songwriter, cowboy singer and motion picture actor. And you would be right.

Hamblen was born into the family of a traveling Methodist preacher on Oct. 20, 1908, in Kellyville, Texas. In later years, after going to Hollywood, he appeared in ten movies with such stars as Roy Rogers, Gene Autry, and John Wayne. He was also a singer and songwriter with his own radio show.

Many of Hamblen's 225 songs were recorded by scores

of artists, not the least of which were Eddy Arnold, Pat Boone, Johnny Cash and Elvis Presley. His song, "This Old House," recorded by Rosemary Clooney, was named Song of the Year in 1954 and was the No. 1 hit song in seven countries at the same time.

In 1949, when Billy Graham was in Los Angeles for evangelist meetings under "The Big Tent," Hamblen's wife persuaded him to attend one of the services. Early the following morning he requested an appointment with Graham - which was granted - and during their conversation Hamblen surrendered his life to be a follower of Christ.

Hamblen tells the story behind one of his songs:

"I wrote the song one night, shortly after midnight. My wife and I had been visiting one of Hollywood's most famous movie stars. We had gone over to his home just to fill him in on some of the things that had happened in his recent absence."

"Somehow the discussion got around to how people can solve problems within themselves. I remember making a statement such as, 'It's no secret what God can do in a man's life.' About two hours later, as we were about to leave the actor's home he said, 'Stuart you ought to write a song about it is no secret what God can do. That is a beautiful thought.'"

"As we walked across the lawn, back to our house, I began to think about it. When we arrived at home, I walked into the living room and sat down at the organ.

Our hall clock began to "chime" the hour of midnight. I grabbed a pen and started writing, 'The chimes of time ring out the news, another day is through' and on and on until the song was finished. I then turned and glanced at the hall clock. It was only 17 minutes after midnight. I could not believe it. I had never been able to write any musical composition in less than three or four hours. I thought the clock had stopped. I then looked and saw the big pendulum still swinging."

Hamblen's song has been heard in every small city, town, and hamlet in America and in countless places around the world - in more than fifty languages. Stuart's neighbor, who suggested writing the song, was John Wayne. You better believe it, pardner!

Printed in the United States
by Baker & Taylor Publisher Services